Workbook One
Of the Business Essentials Series

JOHN MILLAR

Copyright © 2016 John Millar

All rights reserved. No part of this publication may be reproduced, distributed, or transmitted in any form or by any means, including photocopying, recording, or other electronic or mechanical methods, without the prior written permission of the publisher, except in the case of brief quotations embodied in critical reviews and certain other noncommercial uses permitted by copyright law

All rights reserved.

ISBN:1532990464
ISBN-13:9781532990465

DEDICATION

I dedicate this book to my mother and father, who raised me while self-employed. They taught me to work hard and listen to everyone but to make my own choices as to what is right and what is wrong.. and oh, did I mention work hard?

Anyone who tells you to work smart not hard hasn't ever done it tough and realized that if you work smart AND hard you will achieve more than you can possibly dream.

CONTENTS

	Dedication	i
1	Product Description	Pg 6
2	Workbook Content	Pg 7
3	7 Steps to More Profit in Less Time	Pg 28
4	The Business Essentials Series	Pg 31
5	About the Author	Pg 34
6	Client Testimonial	Pg 35

PRODUCT DESCRIPTION

GAINING FOCUS IN YOUR BUSINESS

When you're busy running or managing a business, it's easy to get caught up in the day-to-day tasks.

You become myopic to the expectations, directions and goals you've set and they sit all too comfortably on the long finger of never never.

Rediscovering the basic fundamentals and skills that make a business tick has been a most productive, refreshing and illuminating task for many of our clients. For some, it's a discovery of skills they didn't even know about. Knowing that there are particular ways in which things should be done goes a long way towards smoothing the path for future success.

Moving beyond being simply self-employed, to owning a progressive and innovative business is what this series is all about.

In this DVD you will discover the usefulness goal setting, keeping a time-management diary and transforming your business into a sleek, well-functioning and controlled entity.

So many business owners have expressed such great relief at being able to review this material that we are more convinced than ever of its relevance and value.

Includes 1 DVD Video, 1 CD Audio and Printed PDF Workbook.

To purchase this module go to our website www.moreprofitlesstime.com.

FIRST LET'S TALK ABOUT FOCUS

> When you bump into somebody on an elevator, what have you got prepared to be able to say to them inside 30 seconds that will inspire them to ask you "please tell me more"?

> As we go through the business essential series, it's very important to understand that there is a 4 step process of learning.

The first stage we are initially unconsciously incompetent

The second stage is we then become consciously

The third stage is conscious competency

The fourth the most exciting and also the most dangerous stage is unconscious competence

My philosophy is to make sure that I teach you how to fish

> We will to teach you how to fish for more business, fish for more wealth and fish for how to grow more profit in less time.

> Become far more dissatisfied with where you are at, create a strong and clear vision, identify the steps to achieve your goals.

There was as study done once that if you got a pot of chilled water, or really hot water and drop a frog in it, the frog would jump out straightaway, unfortunately if you put it into a pot of tepid tap water and slowly bring it to the boil that frog will actually stay there and boil to death

> Don't wait till you boil to death

> We see very little of an iceberg above the water, and what we actually see is what others see in the actions that we take and the decisions that we make.

What we don't see below the waterline are all of the beliefs that we generate as we go through our life, the values that we acquire and we apply in their lives and the identity that create as we become more mature individuals and people.

_____
_____
_____
_____
_____

Stop allowing false expectations that appear real to us today to hold us back

_____
_____
_____
_____
_____

How often do you see inside your business the attitude of "Oh, no I couldn't do that, I couldn't allow that change to occur, I am not type of who could do that, we have never done it that way…"

_____
_____
_____
_____

One of the important things to understand that is we've got two hubs to our brain, the left brain and right brain.

_____
_____
_____
_____
_____

GAINING FOCUS IN YOUR BUSINESS

> As we travel through a journey inside your business you'll actually pass numerous sign posts

---

There is a process called VAKOG which is talking about how whether you learn visually, from seeing or A which is auditory so you learn from hearing, K which is Kinesthetically from doing and then more recently, they have discovered areas for development learning you actually find that you can learn from an O which is Olfactory or sense of smell and G, gustatory, so a sense of taste.

VISUAL
AUDITORY
KINAESTHETICALLY
OLFACTORY
GUSTATORY

> Use different colors, different texture, pens, crayons, felt-tip whatever it takes to make those things memorable

---

> Take that I know out of your vocabulary

BFO "Blinding Flashes of the Obvious

> Reticular Activating System or RAS. It's the compass of our brain which allows us to actually notice the things which actually important.

_____
_____
_____
_____
_____

Abraham Lincoln once said "If you give me six hours to chop down a tree, I'll take four hours to sharpen the axe"

_____
_____
_____
_____
_____
_____
_____

In setting a goal, I think there is some very specific areas to be taken into account

_____
_____
_____
_____

The first thing is to look at your direction and focus

_____
_____
_____
_____

The second is setting a goal with a clear outcome

_____
_____
_____
_____
_____

> If you don't have a goal that has both movement and momentum, it just becomes a wish

SPECIFIC
MEASUREABLE
ACHIEVABLE
REALISTIC
TIME BOUND

> If it's not measurable, then how do you know whether you are going to achieve it?

> What are the results you want to achieve?

> In what time frame, are we going to achieve each step and then how do we measure the outcome of that goal?

I believe there are four different components that you must have in your business and plans

The first one is your vision, the second is your mission, the third is your plan and the fourth is the massive action that you must take.

The first one is your vision

The second is your mission

The Third is your Plan

The Fourth is the massive action you must take

Without massive action, you won't achieve massive results

> **Your vision, is not a goal, it's your purpose or intent**

_____
_____
_____
_____
_____

> **What is your purpose and intent of your business?**

_____
_____
_____
_____
_____

> **Why are you in business?**

_____
_____
_____
_____
_____

> Is it purely to make money? Is it to develop an asset that you can pass on to your children? Is to create an asset that you can then sell in, have it as part of your retirement program? Is it to create something that you can actually leave behind as a legacy for the ages that you can be truly proud of?

_____
_____
_____
_____

> **Your company vision, the vision must be something that's almost unattainable. It is something that's way out there.**

_____
_____
_____
_____

> Your vision must enroll and inspire everybody around you, your business partners, your life partners, your children, your team members, your suppliers, your customers. If it doesn't enroll and inspire them, then how they're going to become engaged, and help you to achieve your vision?

What are the core values, by which, your vision is going to be judged?

What is the true purpose for my vision?

What is the envisioned future for my business?

What words would best describe your business?

What qualities would you like to see in your business?

_____
_____
_____
_____

Your mission is the roadmap to the vision, it shows the how to actually getting there, it's the how of what you are going to do to actually achieve that.

_____
_____
_____
_____

Four separate areas you need to cover inside your mission

_____
_____
_____

Who are we?

_____
_____
_____

What business are we really in?

_____
_____
_____

Who are my ideal customers?

_____
_____
_____

What do they look like?

Where do they live?

How old are they?

What sex are they?

What do they like to buy?

What makes us different?

_____
_____
_____
_____
_____
_____

What's the culture inside your business

_____
_____
_____
_____
_____
_____

What are the Rules of the Game?

_____
_____
_____
_____

What are the rules that are acceptable and not acceptable within your business?

_____
_____
_____
_____
_____
_____

First of all, look at the values that are vital to us as people and individuals.

The second, what are the values that are vital to your business succeeding?

Third, what are values that are core to your customers that are buying from you?

Fourth, what are the core values that are important to attain?

Inside your plan you are going to need to have the detail that you need to succeed, the devil is always in the detail.

Think About Your Business

> What does it look like when it's finished?

> Are you looking for a particular sale price, are you looking for particular revenues?

> Does it have you achieving certain level of profits in the business?

> How do you achieve the vision and value within your business?

Working on your business is going to offer you so much more value than just simply working in your business.

> If you haven't allocated the tools and the time to make things happen then the plan merely becomes a dust buster, sits on the shelf and actually doesn't achieve anything.

You need to make sure that you have clarity

Plans need to be both personal and business

You must have a life work balance

How long should those plans be?

Plans should be one year, three year and five year goals that are broken back into individual 90 day plans.

> Make sure that you create a working guide on a weekly basis that follows your plans.

> Your diary is probably one of the most important tools, I really don't care if you use a pocket diary or an electronic diary, most important tools, I really don't care if you use a pocket diary or an electronic diary,

Have a diary to celebrate your successes, celebrate your wins and to make sure that you are on track in everything that you're planning.

Time, it's nonrenewable, you can't get any more of it, all of us have exactly the same amount of it, you need to make the very, very best of what you have.

Time is not the challenge, it's what we do with that allotment of time

If you are not willing to manage your time for yourself, then do it for those that matter in your life!

Who will hold you accountable? Is it your accountant? Is it your book keeper? Is it your business partner? It is your life partner? Do you have a coach or mentor or trainer? Do you actually have a consultant? Do you work with them on a regular basis

---

You need a vision, which is a why

You need a mission, which is a how

You need a plan, which is a what

> You need to take action in a timely manner, which is a when.

> Have you actually understood how a plan falls together?

HI FUN / HI SKILL	HI FUN / LOW SKILL
LOW FUN / HI SKILL	LOW FUN / LOW SKILL

> Make sure that you create your Default Diary.

> You have the choice, to either apply discipline or live with the regret.

> Have you actually finished plans that you've started?

Make sure that you reward yourself every time you achieve your goals!

What are you going to do to recognize and reward your achievements?

> Everything you need to know has probably already been written. It's the new ideas and concepts that come out of that, which enable you to grow and develop as a person and as a professional which then in turn allows you to add value to everyone around you.

If you are not reading, then get over it and check out the book reviews and information we have on our website and blog for recommended reading.

If you have a genuine reading difficulty stop making excuses and buy audio books.

Develop your plan and get clarity on what your vision is.

_____
_____
_____
_____
_____

I'm John Millar, I'm the Managing Director of More Profit Less Time and I appreciate the time that you've given me today, to help you with this critically important process that creates the foundation for you to start building a business creating more profit in less time. Thank you.

John Millar

Here's an example

7 Steps to More Profit Less Time

Area	Current Figure	Areas of Potential	Increase	New Forecast
# of Enquires	4,000	Host Beneficiary Strategic Alliance, Website SEO, Networking Groups	10%	4,400
Conversion %	25%	Defined USP, Quality Guarantee Sales Training, CRM	10%	27.5%
New Customers	1,000			1,210
Retained Customers	2,000	Members Kit, Newsletters Customer Surveys, Loyalty Program	10%	2,200
Total Customers Base	3,000			3,410
Average $ Sale	$100	Increases Prices, Use a checklist Offer Finance, Upsell and Cross Sell	10%	$110
Average of Transactions	2	Have an engaged database, Sell more consumables, Build a relationship	10%	2.2
Total Revenue	$600,000			$825,220
Average GP Margin %	25%	NO DISCOUNTING, Reduce Waste, Negotiate better trading terms, Measure Everything	10%	27.5%
Total Gross Profit	$150,000			$266,935.20
Fixed Costs	$100,000	Better Time Management, Systemize the routine, Reduce Duplication	10%	$90,000
Net Profit	$50,000			$136,935.50

Now it's your turn!

Keep this page blank for photocopying

Business Essentials Series…

Disc 1 in the Business Essentials Series
Gaining Focus in Your Business
This is about your fundamental learning skills and what you will need to do to change them to vastly improve the way you look
at your development to become a truly effective business owner not just simply remain self-employed.

You will also give you some excellent tools to set goals, work on your plans and create a diary that will allow you to steal your time back to begin moving your business from chaos to control.

Disc 2 in the Business Essentials Series
Getting Your Financials Right
You will learn the importance of understanding your financials.

After all being in business is about making profit and having cash flow work for YOU since you are responsible for your profits.
Become your accountant and book keepers best friend by understanding more about how the financials in your business works so you can ask them better questions to maximise your profits not simply ensure tax compliance.

Disc 3 in the Business Essentials Series
Leveraging Your Business Harder
You will learn the principles of what and how to leverage far more in your business to get more from less and to work far smarter and not just harder.

Here is where you will receive some of the tools you will need to better understand how to get your business flying, what it is you need to test and measure, how to do it and WHY it's so important.

Disc 4 in the Business Essentials Series
How to Generate More Clients Profitably
This is where you will determine your uniqueness, develop a meaningful guarantee and learn the basics of good advertising.

You will gain a better appreciation between the difference of Marketing and Advertising, learn how to get the most for the least investment and ensure that you do it all profitably.

Disc 5 in the Business Essentials Series
Maximising Your Conversion Rates
Get to know how your Sales Pipeline REALLY works and how to identify who your suspects really are, convert prospects into regular shoppers and understand how much more work you can do to maximise your sales experience.

Disc 6 in the Business Essentials Series
Meet and Exceed Your Clients Expectations

Now you have new customers, how do you make sure you KEEP them, how do you wanting to come back time and again while telling their friends? ...this is where you really make a difference.

Disc 7 in the Business Essentials Series
Systemising Your Business For Consistent Excellence
Do you recognise the importance of having systems in your business and how they can improve your profitability?

We show you how to systemise like a corporate while retaining the culture of a smaller business. Understanding how we systemise for routine and humanise for the exceptions will enable you to be the best in your field every time.

Disc 8 in the Business Essentials Series
Do You Have a Champion Team with a Champion Leader?
This is about having the right people on the bus. It starts with you however so you'll learn how to maximise your own skills and then you will attract and retain the right people.

When you understand how the TEAM is the most important part of your business and what needs to be done to achieve the very best from yourselves and others you are well on your way to becoming a better manager of this invaluable resource.

Disc 9 in the Business Essentials Series
The Essentials of Getting Your Time Back.
This is where you get to redefine your time management You will understand better how you can start working far more on the business than in the business than ever before.

You will also finally find out why others can seem to fit more into their day while having a great LIFE – WORK balance (notice the order!)..

Disc 10 in the Business Essentials Series
Simply Brilliant Customer Service.
It's so easy to give mediocre or good customer service but it's just as easy to give amazing service to your customers and delight them.

You will understand the simple easy steps that you must take to provide consistently brilliant service and how to get your team excited about doing it.

Disc 11 in the Business Essentials Series
Discovering DISC and EQ not just IQ.
We believe for things to change first you must change so here you will learn why you behave as you do and just as importantly understand why other people react and act the way they do.

You will also learn what DISC really is and what it isn't. You will learn how to apply these important principles in your recruitment and team management / development.

You will learn how to use these ideas in creating a more dynamic team and discover the what and why of emotional intelligence. You will also develop key strategies for using the knowledge here and the tools we have available on our website and why we place such a massive emphasis on DISC and other tools that support, train and develop your team.

You will also learn how to use these skills and observations at home and socially not just at the workplace.

Disc 12 in the Business Essentials Series
Quality Recruitment.
Recruitment of the right people for the right reasons in the right roles for your team is so incredibly important yet so often ignored or pushed to the rear.

You will learn who the right person is for your business and the role you want filled.
You will be able to identify the right people early in the process to save yourself and them the time and money wasted with antique recruitment methodologies that just don't work anymore.

How to get the best out of your recruitment activities so you can keep the assets you acquire for the long term and get the best return from your investment.

ABOUT THE AUTHOR

John Millar is the Managing Director, Senior Business Coach Trainer and Consultant with More Profit Less Time Pty Ltd and CEO-ONDEMAND. Along with his many other business interests, John is proud to have been an associate of the most successful coaching team in the world.

He is recognized as a global leader and has been benchmarked against over 1,300 colleagues in 31 countries. John has over 25 years of hands-on ownership, management, coaching, and entrepreneurial experience in a broad range of industry sectors, including retail, wholesale, import, export, IT, trades and trade services, automotive, primary production, food services, transport, manufacturing, mining, professional services, the fitness industry, and more.

He has extensive experience developing and providing training for small to medium-sized companies and a variety of publicly listed corporate companies. John is an accomplished and talented public and professional speaker. He has been a mentor working with sales/management activities for businesses with a turnover under $100,000 per annum, over $100 million turnover, and everything in between, with great success.

John currently works with business owners and their teams across Australia and has a "Whatever it takes" attitude that has enabled him to help his clients grow their business profits by up to 800%.

 If you are ready to be coached by one of the best in the business, register at:

www.ceo-ondemand.com.au

Make sure to visit www.moreprofitlesstime.com for the new online Management Development Program: The Business Essentials Series.

ACCLAIM FOR JOHN MILLAR'S
Business Coaching and Training in their own words...

"Without John Millar as my Business Coach I wouldn't have a business today."—Grant Jennings Managing Director, Jigsaw Projects

"Taking the decision to be coached and trained by John Millar was carefully considered after experiencing those who over promised and under delivered. I am pleased to say the content of his courses are the tools we all need to master as business owners. His delivery is engaging, thought provoking and empowering and after every session l came away re-energised. John always makes himself available for business building advice both via Skype and face to face beyond the scope of delivery. With his extensive personal experience in building small businesses, he knows and understands what it takes to establish and grow a business.I have no hesitation endorsing John Millar as an educator and business coach and the bonus is he is a very nice person."—Anne Lederman Managing Director FB Salons"

Johns training with my management team was excellent, it was very different from the business coaching and support I have had in the past. John was clear, thoughtful and he addressed the issues we needed to cover without us even knowing they were being addressed! His follow up has been fantastic and exactly what I needed. I would recommend John and his team to anyone looking at getting some business coaching and training done" —Wendy Crawford, Peopleworx

"In my dealings with John as our business coach, I have found him to be a motivated and insightful agent of positive change. He is able to burrow down to the root cause of issues and introduce effective forms of measurement. John then identifies and implements practical solutions and is there to provide the gentle persuasion required to ensure that results are achieved." —Mark Felton, Lindale Insurances

"You have coached and trained us so well throughout the year that we are now used to & find it easy to prepare a 90 day plan, then breaks it down to actionable bite size pieces. Planning in business & personal life certainly is important. It allows us to identify the important things & the bigger picture. Thank you for your support & guidance throughout the year. And not to mention your insight, external perspective to review & assist our business moving forward." —Linda Turner, Director Roy A McDonald Certified Practicing Accountants

"If you want to achieve sales results you never thought were possible and give yourself a competitive edge my strong suggestion is to engage John services and listen closely to what John has to say, during the time I was trained by John I was one of eight sales consultants in a national business for 10 out of the 13 months I lead the sales tally and in 1 quarter I generated three times the revenue of the national sales force combined. Johns training and experience was well worth the investment and paid big dividends. Thanks John." —Julian Fadini, Bellvue Capital

"John is a very enthusiastic trainer and business coach, he is very passionate about getting business owners and their team where they need to be. He goes the extra mile to keep ahead of the latest developments which he then uses to benefit his clients." —Darren Reddy CPA

"I have been to a few seminars and heard John speak numerous times about sales, marketing and business. He is a very knowledgable and extremely enthusiastic business coach in all his interactions and I would recommend him to all business owners who need a sales and marketing boost!" —Andrew Heath, Managing Director, Fresh Living Group

"I worked with John Millar and found his business knowledge, passion and innovation to be inspiring. He has always been able to set (and achieve) strategic long and short-term goals both for himself and his clients without losing that personal connection he builds with everyone he meets. He has been and I believe will continue to be a strong mentor and trainer for anyone wanting to take that next step in their business." —Bree Webster, Online Marketing Guru

"Massive Action Day" – what an understatement, John Millars 4 hour frenzy challenged me to seriously review areas of my business I would not have gone to …. In this way, the process identified incongruence's in my mind, my business and my modus operandi. It's created a paradigm shift. Thanks John, the road map just got a whole lot clearer. Your friendship and insights since 2003 have been a gift to my business and I." —Andrew Reay, Counsellor, Hypnotherapist and Counsellor, Thinkshift Transformations

"John Millar is not your usual Business coach or trainer; he gets involved with you and your business and provides hands on help to make sure you follow through on his advice. He is highly motivated to help his clients and his personal guarantee certainly shows this. He has now transposed his thoughts, advice and love of good business onto a series of DVD's in his business venture – More Profit Less Time. This has excellent tips and advice for anyone either starting out or already in business. I highly recommend John to any business owner who wants to run a business and not a j.o.b.!" —Darren Cassidy, Managing Director HR2U

"I and many of my Business Partners and colleagues have worked with John since 2010 as our business oath, trainer and motivator and found him to be an extremely motivational person to assist us achieve our business goals. This company and its products allows for John's skill set to be accessed by a wider number of potential clients. His very professional DVD series is extremely good value for money and is easily accessible for all of us who are time poor. If you are looking to maximise your and your business's results and to start achieving your goals and dreams, contact John; you won't look back!!" —Mark Cleland, Mortgage Choice

"John develops real relationships with the people he comes into contact with. He is pasionate about what he does. His DVD and group training series, is full of good ideas and process to make your business better. Knowing what to do and actually doing it are two different things. John is excellent at helping you get things done." —Carey Rudd, Sales Director, Online Knowledge

"I have known John since 2004 and found him to be extremely knowledgably in both Sales and Business systems as a business coach without peer. John has provided me with business advice as well as personal coaching over the years, helping me with the running of my organisation. I'm impressed with John's DVD series where he has condensed a lot of the information in an easy to follow format that any business owner can use immediately. I wish he had released these DVDs earlier, as they are a goldmine of information, and practical how to that allow anyone to increase the profit in their business and get back valuable wasted time." —Steve Psaradellis, Managing Director, TEBA

"John's DVD and workbook delivery of his no-nonsense advice provides a low-cost option for those business owners looking to set and achieve goals that will increase profit. I found the conversational style of the DVD's easy to follow, whilst the requirement to pause the DVD and write down some action points ensured a level of commitment to the advice being provided." — Mark Felton, Lindale Insurances

"I only met John briefly at a BNI meeting and knew instantly i need to hire him for my business as my business coach. His attitude towards work and how to improve my cash line had an instant effect on before, even before I finally hired him on an official basis. I found myself thinking "what would John do" and this was only after just meeting him. I cannot see my business expend and give me "More Profit Less Time" without John's expert direction and training. If you want to succeed in business life, you need John Millar, without him you're just kidding yourself " —Leslie Cachia, Managing Director, Letac Drafting

"I can highly recommend John Millar to any business owner who wants to grow his business. When I hear very positive feedback from colleagues who are skeptics by nature about John's ability and skills, I know John will help all those he comes in contact with. John comes with a selfless nature and the willingness to work inside a client's business to make it succeed. Rare indeed!" —Darren Cassidy, Managing Director, HR2U"I first met John Millar in mid-2010 and have always found him to be of an honest and generous character that engenders an easy association with him. I love how easy he is to listen to and how passionate he is about his work and topics. John demonstrates a love for life and his work and I have no hesitation in recommending his services." —Kathie M Thomas, Managing Director, VA

"I have listened to John speak on a number of occasions and find him a very knowledgeable speaker with a passion for what he does. I have also interacted with a number of his clients and they all tell me that he helps them achieve results in their business. If you are looking for business help John is a person you can trust." —Carey Rudd, Sales Director, Online Knowledge

"John knows his stuff, he knows how the get results, John has so many great ideas in building a business and helping business owners work less and make more money. John has released a DVD set on doing just that. I have watched the 1st one and it was great, very informative and easy to understand, I happily recommend John to anyone in need of help and guidance" —Frank Eramo, Proprietor, Dynotune

"I have known John only for a short time, however the impact that he has had on me, not just my business has helped me to visualise opportunities that I began to doubt my ability to realise. He is encouraging and at the same time challenging so that he can/you can, begin to see how to maximise the business potential, John calls it being an unreasonable friend, I call it being a mate. If you have any questions about the direction of your business, if you want to seem your bottom line improve not just turnover but real profit, if you want a person who will work with you then I strongly recommend that you engage him at your earliest convenience. John is the best thing that has happened to my business. I could tell you about the way he is on track to make 1/2 a million for me on his contacts alone, but that actually sells him short, he has become like my partner in business, and cares about my success as if it was his own, we will flourish because I took the step to employ his training to help me grow. If you get a chance to get him training you, don't wait like I did, get in as quickly as possible, his time is your business and if like me your business is to make money, then every day you don't have him on retainer you lose money." —Russell Summers, Managing Director, The Give Life Centre

"It's usually easy to be mediocre in business but it's impossible when you have John Millar training you. He has been my right hand since 2003!" —David Manser, CFO, Hydrosteer

"I now have a commercial, profitable business and now it's my choice when I work IN my business and when I work ON it and have had john helping me in business since 1988. I can't imagine not having John as a part of our business." —David Wall, Director, D&K Transport

"The work John has done since 2008 coaching and training our marketing team, administration and finance teams, buyers, store managers and staff nationally have been fantastic." —Ross Sudano, Director, Anaconda Adventure Stores

"John is a creative, professional, practical and committed business coach and trainer. His approach since we first met him in 1994 to working with a client team through the application of useful tools, information and anecdotes along with his easy going & easy to understand delivery sets him apart from other business coaches that I have used in the past." —Anthony Beasley, Director, The Astra Group

"I have worked with John Millar for the since 2004 and I didn't think it was possible to achieve what we have achieved together. His business coaching, training and services just get better and better!" —Terrance Chong, Managing Director, Echo Graphics and Printing

"John's business coaching, training and support has transformed our business across Australia and New Zealand since 2008."—Rose Vis, Managing Director, VIP Australia

"We first met John in 2005, he is AMAZING at sales, marketing, operations, logistics, finance training and so much more. Since engaging John as our business coach our business has exploded, our team are happy, our clients are raving about us and my husband and I now take at least 12 weeks holidays a year, EVERY year." —Shirley Du, Director, Goldline Technology

"It's the no nonsense results driven business coaching and training focus John bought to the table that had such a massive effect on our business." —David Runkel, Director, Tracomp Fabrication and Steel

"We started working with John in early 2010, within 90 days of working with and being trained by John Millar we had the biggest and most profitable month in our 15 year history. That's impressive." —Hugh Gilchrist, Managing Director, Australian Moulding Company

"If you don't have John as your business trainer you aren't meeting your business potential." —Don Robertson, Director, Medallion Electrical Services

Thank You!